CLASSIC *f*M

Land of Hope and Glory

A Festival of Epic British Music

Arranged for intermediate piano by Barrie Carson Turner

Contents

*Arranged by Pam Wedgwood
**Arranged by Peter Gritton

Faber Music in association with Classic FM, a Global Radio station.
Faber Music is the exclusive print publisher for all Global Radio sheet music product.

© 2010 Faber Music Ltd
First published in 2010 by Faber Music Ltd
Bloomsbury House 74–77 Great Russell Street London WC1B 3DA
Music processed by Jeanne Roberts
Introduction by Julian Haylock
Printed in England by Caligraving Ltd
All rights reserved

ISBN10: 0-571-53479-1
EAN13: 978-0-571-53479-1

To buy Faber Music/Global Radio publications, or to find out about the full range of titles available,
please contact your local retailer, or go to www.fabermusic.com or www.classicfm.com/shop.
For sales enquiries, contact Faber Music at sales@fabermusic.com or tel: +44 (0)1279 828982.

Foreword

There is something very inspiring about British Festival Music,

simply because many pieces were composed for celebration.

The unique arrangements available within this book allow a pianist

to capture the essence and occasion of those rousing orchestral works.

My highlights include **Rule Britannia** (Arne), **Jerusalem** (Parry), and

I Vow to Thee, My Country (Holst). Once you've mastered the pieces,

why not get some friends over for a sing-along?

John Brunning, Classic FM

The Classic FM Full Works album 'Land of Hope and Glory' (CFMFW070)
is available now exclusively at HMV.

Introduction

This bracing collection of British classics features some of the finest celebratory music ever composed, opening with Walton's **Crown Imperial** (1937), the product of a nation enjoying the last vestiges of Edwardian pomp and ceremony in the grand Elgarian style. Just as surely as *Orb and Sceptre* unerringly caught the new mood of optimism following the ravages of the Second World War, *Crown Imperial*, composed for the coronation of King George VI, feels in retrospect like a final majestic musical statement of a society whose very fabric would soon be torn asunder. It was originally played at the point in the ceremony when the Queen Mother entered the building – a grand welcome indeed.

Parry, the doyen of English late-Romantic composers, originally composed his ceremonial anthem **I Was Glad** for the coronation of King Edward VII in 1902. He later revised it for the coronation of King George V in 1911, when he added the glorious organ introduction familiar from performances today. The work's majestic opening phrases ultimately make way for an intensely moving prayer for peace.

Gustav Holst's posthumous reputation rests almost entirely on one blazingly inspired work – *The Planets* (1914-16). This sublime masterpiece of celestial portraiture remains the ultimate musical guide to the solar system, yet Holst apparently never thought all that highly of it. Cast in seven movements, each depicts one of the then-known planets except Earth (Pluto wasn't discovered until 1930). 'Jupiter, the Bringer of Jollity' contrasts two irrepressibly lively outer sections with a broad central melody, popularly sung to the words **I Vow to Thee, My Country.**

Stanford was a highly-skilled composer of symphonies, piano concertos, string quartets and sonatas, yet his finest work is to be found in his choral music, including the soaring *Blue Bird*, the exquisite Latin motet *Beati quorum via*, and his **Songs of the Sea** (1904), a setting of five poems by his friend, the then poet laureate, Sir Henry Newbolt, for baritone solo and orchestra. Two of the songs are included here as piano arrangements: **Drake's Drum,** celebrating the life of Sir Francis Drake, the man who triumphed over the Spanish Armada in 1588, and **The Old Superb**, which refers to Nelson's continual hounding of the French fleet, which led eventually to the Battle of Trafalgar.

Elgar's *'Enigma' Variations* (1899) is effectively a series of character portraits dedicated 'To my friends pictured within'. The cryptic headings that head each variation in the score were successfully decoded long ago – the ravishing **Nimrod** variation, included here, alludes to Elgar's publisher, Jaeger (German for 'hunter', hence the Biblical 'Nimrod').

Arguably the most gifted light-music composer England has ever produced, Eric Coates started out life as a viola player in several distinguished orchestras and string quartets. However, from 1919 he devoted himself exclusively to producing a stream of indelible classics in every miniature form of the day, from suites and ballets to overtures, serenades, more than 100 songs, and countless marches, including *The Dambusters*, *Calling all Workers* and **Knightsbridge March**. The latter was later adapted as a signature tune for BBC Radio's *In Town Tonight* programme, which prompted a remarkable 20,000 listeners' letters demanding to know the composer's name!

During the coronation of Queen Elizabeth II, Walton's choral *Te Deum* was sung towards the end of the ceremony following the blessing as the Queen made her way to St Edward's Chapel, where she was presented with a robe of purple velvet, the imperial crown and her orb and sceptre. As she made her way back towards the West door of the Abbey, another stirring piece filled the building with glorious sound – Walton's exuberant, celebratory march **Orb and Sceptre**, also written especially for the occasion. Not since Handel composed his four coronation anthems for George II had a newly-crowned monarch enjoyed such a spectacular musical welcome.

Borrowing the title from a phrase in Shakespeare's *Othello*, Elgar composed his first of five **Pomp and Circumstance** Marches in 1901. Little did he know that the central melody would soon rival *God Save the Queen* in popularity – particularly when sung to the words of Laurence Housman's *Land of Hope and Glory*. After conducting the first Promenade performance, Sir Henry Wood reported: 'The people simply rose and yelled. I had to play it again – with the same result... Merely to restore order, I played the march a third time.'

Six years earlier the same conductor had raised his baton on 10 August 1895 for the start of the first in a series of 'promenade concerts'. He could hardly have envisaged the impact this would have, not only on the rest of his professional life but on the musical culture of the entire nation. Remarkably, Wood (later 'Sir Henry') would go on to devise and conduct virtually every promenade concert for the next 50 years, often including his own **Fantasia on British Sea Songs**, which has become a regular fixture ever since.

Sometimes seen as an anthem for the English, **Jerusalem** was set to music by Parry in 1916 and made such an impact that Elgar himself made a stunning orchestration of it. Three main theories prevail regarding the reference to 'dark, satanic mills' (verse 1). To some it is a protest at the ravages of early industrialisation on England's landscape. Later research suggests it may be a veiled reference to the Anglican Church, or even to the 'dreaming spires' of the Oxford and Cambridge skylines.

Another popular favourite during the 'Last Night' of the Proms, **Rule Britannia** was the unforgettable inspiration of Thomas Arne (1710-1778) who first included it in his 1740 theatrical masque, *Alfred*. Arne was an enormously prolific composer, whose tally of stage works ran to over 100, including seven based on Shakespeare alone. In addition he wrote many songs, odes, cantatas, sonatas, overtures, catches, canons, glees, symphonies and some ballet music, yet he appears destined to be remembered almost exclusively for this indefatigable outburst of chest-beating patriotism.

Crown Imperial

William Walton
(1902–1983)

I Vow To Thee, My Country

from *The Planets* Suite

Gustav Holst
(1874–1934)

Rule Britannia

Thomas Arne
(1710–1778)

Nimrod

from the 'Enigma' Variations Op.36

Edward Elgar
(1857–1934)

Orb and Sceptre

Molto espressivo e sostenuto

William Walton
(1902–1983)

I Was Glad

Hubert Parry
(1848–1918)

Knightsbridge March

from the *London Suite*

Eric Coates
(1886–1957)

Jerusalem

Hubert Parry
(1848–1918)

Slow, with movement

Drake's Drum

from *Songs of the Sea* Op.91

Poems by Sir Henry Newbolt

Charles Villiers Stanford
(1852–1924)

Tempo di marcia moderato

The Old Superb

from *Songs of the Sea* Op.91

Poems by Sir Henry Newbolt

Charles Villiers Stanford
(1852–1924)

Fantasia on British Sea Songs

Music Traditional
Arranged by Henry Joseph Wood

Pomp and Circumstance
Op.39, March No.1

Edward Elgar
(1857–1934)

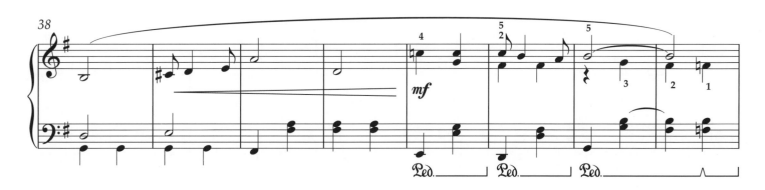

con Ped.

Maestoso ♩ = 80

Land of hope and glo - ry Mo - ther of the free

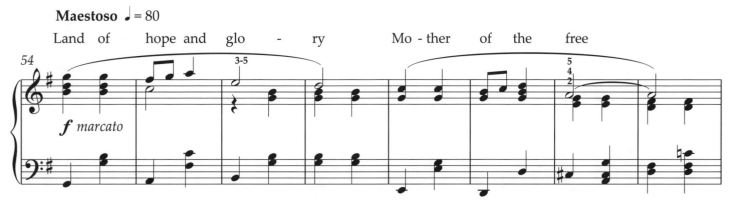

How shall we ex - tol thee who are born of thee?

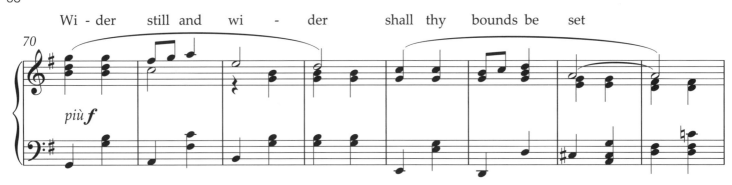

Wi - der still and wi - der shall thy bounds be set

God who made thee migh - ty make thee migh - tier yet

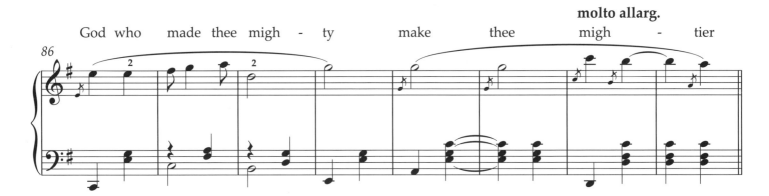

God who made thee migh - ty make thee migh - tier

As fast as possible ♩ = c.120

yet!

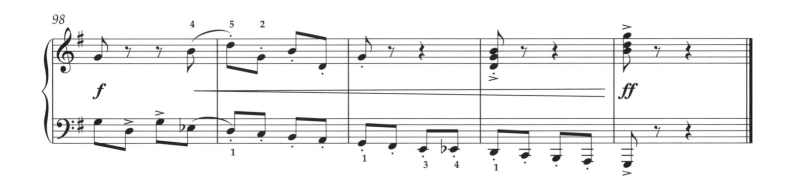

Real Repertoire Piano

Including pieces ranging from JS Bach's Invention in F *to Peter Maxwell Davies'* Farewell to Stromness

0-571-52119-3

Baroque Real Repertoire

Including JS Bach's Invention in A minor, *Purcell's* A New Ground *and Paradies'* Toccata

0-571-52333-1

Classical Real Repertoire

Including Beethoven's Bagatelles in D *and* E flat, *Hummel's* To Alexis *and* Schubert's Moment Musical in F minor

0-571-52334-X

Romantic Real Repertoire

Including Chopin's Waltz in C sharp minor, *Field's* Nocturne in B flat *and* Fauré's Romance sans paroles

0-571-52335-8

Twentieth Century Real Repertoire

Including Bartók's Melody in the Mist, *Debussy's* The Little Shepherd *and* Sculthorpe's Evening Star *and* Singing Sun

0-571-52336-6

Christine Brown (editor)

To buy Faber Music publications or to find out about the full range of titles available
please contact your local music retailer or Faber Music sales enquiries:

Faber Music Ltd, Burnt Mill, Elizabeth Way, Harlow CM20 2HX
Tel: +44 (0) 1279 82 89 82   Fax: +44 (0) 1279 82 89 83
sales@fabermusic.com   fabermusic.com   expressprintmusic.com